PERSONAL VILLAGE®

WORKBOOK

Six Steps To Build Your Personal Community

Marvin Thomas, MSW

Lakeridge Press
Seattle

Published by
Lakeridge Press
P.O. Box 27645
Seattle, WA 98165-2645
(206) 364-9494
www.personalvillage.com

Copyright © 2006 by Marvin Thomas, MSW

All rights reserved. No part of this book may be reproduced in any form or by any means electronic or mechanical, including photocopying, recording or by any information storage and retrieval systems, without written permission of the publisher or author except where permitted by law.

Printed in the United States of America
10 9 8 7 6 5 4 3 2

ISBN-10: 0-9772783-1-X
ISBN-13: 978-0-9772783-1-2

Cover Layout Design by Tami Taylor
Cover Artwork by Iskra Johnson
Interior Book Design by Tami Taylor

This book is dedicated to
Swami Chidvilasananda

Table of Contents

Acknowledgments   3

Introduction   4

How To Use This Book   5

What Is A Personal Village?   6

Why We All Need A Strong Personal Village In Today's World   7

How To Get The Most Out Of This Course   10

How To Gain The Most From Your Study Group Experience   12

How To Gain The Most From The Individual Self Study Process   14

Guardianship   16

The Importance Of Warm-up   17

    1st Session—Defining The Personal Village   19

    2nd Session—Shaping Your Personal Village   33

    3rd Session—Roaming As An Art   39

    4th Session —Meeting People   47

    5th Session—Building Friendships: Mapping Your Village   55

    6th Session—Pulling Your Personal Village Together   65

What To Do Next   69

Community Fulfillment Test   71

Acknowledgments

Behind every book stands a host of people who have contributed to the wisdom the author hopes to express. Standing behind the creation of this workbook are the legions of students and seekers who have taught me more about the inner life of the human heart than I ever believed was possible. For the last four decades, they have been teaching me how to listen, how to appreciate the eagerness of sincere seekers, and how to hold the sacred vessel of vitality that swirls in every human gathering. This book is their gift to you and to them I owe everything that I have learned.

I have no words to express the great gratitude that I hold for Peggy, my wife of 45 years. She has been one of the great teachers in my life and has been a steady presence standing by my side as I struggled to find a way to create a language about Personal Village that could be understood by anyone. She is my rock.

This book was not written as a solo project by me. Standing in the wings was the production team that nudged, encouraged, and guided the creation of this book from a mere idea into a finished work. Jennifer McCord has been my muse, associate, and consultant from the time I first became serious about writing this series. She has taken the role of developmental editor, publishing consultant, and best of all, a good friend. Tami Taylor is a jewel of a woman who designed the cover and did the layout for the book. She is the genius that lingers out of sight making sure all the artistic and technical details are just right. Her skill and steady hand is a great blessing to me personally. Gloria Campbell helped develop the concept of this book as a teaching tool and worked steadily with me throughout every step. Her gentle touch as an editor is a rare gift for which I am very appreciative.

In the background stand the ancestors who are the real authors of this Personal Village material. Though most of them are no longer alive, they were my parents and grandparents, teachers, colleagues, and early developers of the "personal network" concept, as it was long called. Carolyn Attneve was a psychologist, teacher, and writer who brought her native American Indian wisdom about the value of community into modern thinking. She worked closely with me as I initially developed the Personal Village ideas. Her fingerprints are everywhere in this work. She was a grand woman. Leon Fine was my mentor about the fine points of group dynamics. I often hear his voice when I am leading groups and appreciate the great lessons he passed onto me. And, finally, I honor Jacob Moreno who before World War II flagged the importance of personal circles of people as the only way that we will be able to survive our leap into modern technological society. His pioneering work stands behind this effort.

Introduction

After releasing *Personal Village—How To Have People In Your Life by Choice, Not Chance*, I have conducted many workshops and seminars which have tested and provided the basic skills needed to make the Personal Village concept come alive. Many requests have come for an additional book that would contain the steps outlined in those workshops. This workbook is intended to address that need.

The process laid out here will not only help you learn about community, it will also provide a transformative experience that is intended to develop community-building skills into the very core of your being.

After working with these steps, you will have as deep a familiarity with your Personal Village as you have about everything else that makes your life work—the skills needed to drive a car, to read and write, to raise children, and to be successful at your work.

This workbook is intended to serve as a self-study guide for both individuals who want or need to take this course alone and those who want to use it as a guide in a small study group. It can also be adapted by a teacher to a classroom setting.

Tending your Personal Village is a lifelong process. These skills will continue to grow throughout your life. This workbook will give you the language of community, start you thinking about your Personal Village, and introduce you to the skills you will need as you go forward. Though these six steps will not teach you everything you will need to know, they will give you a flying start.

My life mission is to enhance a sense of community for as many people as I can reach. I offer this book with the prayer that you will envelop yourself in a rich surround of community, a community that nourishes you and contributes to your life, a community of people that you, in turn, care for and nourish. May your Personal Village truly become one of the greatest treasures of your life.

How To Use This Book

Working through the steps described in this book will require discipline. In most courses, a teacher is present to lead the way, to set the tone and provide focus, to watch the time and move us from one activity to another. In this course, no one will be there to do this for you. So, if you want to get the most out of this book, it will be up to you to be your own teacher. That means you will need to carefully read the material that precedes each step. And as you progress through the six sessions, it will be important to follow the instructions so this course will bear fruit.

This workbook is written to stand by itself; however, you will gain more if you use it in concert with the primary text, *Personal Village—How To Have People In Your Life by Choice, Not Chance*. Many ideas will be introduced and briefly described in the workbook, but if you want a richer experience, study the suggested chapters in the primary text as well.

Since this workbook is about community, the best way to learn and apply the material is in the company of others. If you want to learn how to swim, you need to get into the water. If you want to learn about community, you need to immerse yourself in a community. If you can find a small study group to work with, your learning will be more lasting and meaningful.

If you do not have a small group available, you can substitute journaling and contemplation for the group sessions. Eventually, however, you will need to take your growing understanding out into the sea of people who make up your life.

Every part of this book, from the material on how to get the most out of this course to the individual activities in the six sessions, is designed to provide the basic skills you will need as you build your own Personal Village. If you apply yourself to the material, you will learn how to carefully tend your relationships. Your success will depend totally on the amount of effort you expend.

This book will also become your personal journal about community building. You may want to keep it private until after you have finished the course. Then you can decide if you want to share it with others.

Be sure to write your name in the front of the book and date it. In the future, you will be curious about how you saw your Personal Village at this point in your life.

What Is A Personal Village?

No matter where you live, you are surrounded by a village—a village that contains all of the people who make up the fabric of your life. It is not a village of thatched roofs, cows, and dusty roads. It is a human village that contains everyone who shelters you with warmth, caring, security, and a sense of belonging and purpose.

Your Personal Village means everyone that you know. That means you know most of their names and they know your name, and that you have some kind of interaction and common ground upon which you walk. It is unique to you. It is the very foundation of your life, and it is one of the most important assets you will ever have.

Why is it so important?

Everything you need to live your life to its fullest potential involves people. Family births and raises you. Teachers educate you. Friends and colleagues provide support on your career path. Fellow seekers accompany you on your spiritual journey. Professionals provide health care and financial guidance.

The inherent drive to become the greatest you are capable of being is dependent upon teachers, colleagues, and friends. And ultimately you will depend upon caregivers and family to provide support as you age. Without people in your Personal Village, life would not be possible.

Your village exists not only to serve you. You are also there to serve and tend it. Caring and giving go both ways in an effective personal community.

If your village is sparse, your life will probably be lacking and empty. If, on the other hand, you succeed in filling your village with a host of supportive people, your life will be rich and full. There is a one-to-one correlation between the strength of your Personal Village and the success of your life.

Why We All Need A Strong Personal Village In Today's World

You know the African proverb that it takes a village to raise a child. The deeper truth is that it takes a village to support you on your life journey from birth to death. These are the people you know personally and they know you personally. You know each other's names and much about your mutual lives. Whenever anyone in this village needs something, they can immediately turn to you or others for any resource. This process has been going on in our walk-around neighborhoods for hundreds of thousands of years. It was going on in the savanna land in Africa. It was going on in the jungles of South America and in the neighborhoods of Chicago and every other city and town. People have depended upon each other for so long that it has become embedded in our genetic code. Community is at the heart of what it is to be human.

About 100 years ago we stopped walking around in our people world. The trains were beginning to run, the telephone was invented, then came the automobile and airplanes and, now, instant messaging. Suddenly, everything on the planet became available to us. We eagerly embraced this new boon and our lives improved immensely. But, in the process, too many of us forgot something very important—the people in our lives.

For example, take two women, Louise and Emily. They were neighbors and very good friends. Every day they sat in each other's homes and talked about the kids, the town, their families, and shared child care. Spending time in each other's company stimulated endorphin, a beneficial hormone that made them both happier and healthier. When Louise needed a pie pan she walked over to Emily's for an hour of conversation before returning home with the pan. This face-to-face time gave each of them an endorphin boost, reinforced their sense of belonging and feeling of being valued by another person.

Then came the telephone. Now Louise could simply call Emily and ask if her pie pan was free. Emily said, "Of course," and Louise said, "Good, I will send Johnny over to get it." The endorphin boost and personal affirmation dropped a notch.

Then cars arrived. Now Louise did not need to call Emily. She could hop in the car and drive to the store to buy her own pie pan. The endorphin boost was disappearing. The relationship between these two women was thinning out.

Today when Louise needs a pie pan she can go to the Internet and order a pie from *Pies On The Fly*. Soon a whole pie is delivered out of the back of a van by a stranger. Louise and Emily no longer need each other for pie pans and their relationship suffers or, perhaps, disappears altogether. No more emotional nourishment. No more affirmation. No more endorphin benefit from being in each other's company. They both suffer.

Technology and modern life have speeded things up, replaced people with services, and separated us in time and distance. The attempt to remain connected electronically meets some of our needs, but does not address our genetic need to spend time in the physical company of others. Our health suffers. We are not as mentally and emotionally healthy. The stress hormones generated by our fast-paced life no longer are balanced by the refuge of good company. The Personal Villages that we are genetically encoded to live within have become less central to our lives.

This fast-paced world has no vested interest in having us connected with others. No profits are made from people hanging out together. Instead, we are encouraged to turn to high tech instruments, merchandise, and anonymous services from which others make money. We become stressed by hurrying to one exciting activity after another and reaching for satisfaction by buying and embracing another great technological wonder. The absence of a beneficial Personal Village is of no concern to investors.

The true pathway to fulfillment and success runs right through the middle of our Personal Villages. If we are to restore our genetic need to be surrounded by people, we will have to slow down and make it happen ourselves. This course will teach you how to do just that.

You may want to stop right now and take a little survey to see if or how much you need to attend to your Personal Village.

Take this brief survey to see if you need to strengthen your Personal Village:

1. Do you have all the people you want in your life?

   ❏ Yes   ❏ I want more   ❏ No, I am lonely

2. Do you feel sufficiently skilled to create a sense of community for yourself?

   ❏ Yes   ❏ I wish I knew more   ❏ No, I don't know what to do

3. Do you have adequate time in your schedule to spend time with the people who are important to you?

   ❏ Yes   ❏ Kind of   ❏ No

4. Does your personal community have people who would care if you got sick or were in need?

   ❏ Yes   ❏ Not enough   ❏ No

5. Do you have several people you know well enough to ask them to get out of bed in the middle of the night to come to your aid?

   ❏ Yes   ❏ I wish I had more   ❏ No

6. Do you have someone in your life who really knows who you are?

   ❏ Yes   ❏ I feel kind of known   ❏ No

7. Do you have the level of personal intimacy with someone that gives your life a sense of fullness?

   ❏ Yes   ❏ Only in part   ❏ No

8. After engaging with people all day, do you feel satisfied and fulfilled?

   ❏ Yes   ❏ Yes and No   ❏ No

9. Do you have all the people you want in your life who can help to make it go more smoothly? For example, do you know folks who know the name of a good doctor or a hairdresser?

   ❏ Yes   ❏ Not enough   ❏ No

If you answered yes to most of these questions, your Personal Village is probably working well and taking this course will ensure it stays that way. If you answered in the middle or no to most of these questions, you will benefit from going through this workbook. That will help to strengthen your Personal Village.

How To Get The Most Out Of This Course

If you can, read the first two chapters of the primary text, *Personal Village—How to Have People in Your Life by Choice, Not Chance*, before you start. Although you can take the course without reading that text, you will gain much more if you read it as you go through the six steps.

In order to prevent confusion between the workbook and the book, I will refer to *Personal Village — How To Have People In Your Life by Choice*, Not Chance as the "primary text." The Personal Village Workbook will be called the "workbook."

If you are meeting with a study group, decide in advance how often you will meet. Weekly or every other week sessions are the most beneficial. You can meet less frequently, but you will lose ground because it will take too long at the beginning of each session to get started again.

If you are working alone with a journal, doing a session more often than once a week will not allow you enough time to digest the material. You need to let the ideas soak in before you move to the next session.

If you work with a group, you can become so interested in each other's lives that it will be tempting to drift away from the study plan laid out in the book. Make it a practice to keep to the times and topics as laid out and save other questions and sharing for outside of class. If you are not careful about this, you will spend so much time on outside issues that you will never get around to the meat of the course.

Be on time. Latecomers disrupt the class for everyone. Your absence during the opening minutes will be keenly felt by everyone and will distract from the rest of the session. Waiting for a late member feels like an anchor that is dragging a boat that is trying to get underway. For some people, being late is a pattern. If you are a habitual late-arriver, you may do others a favor by taking this course individually.

Of course, unavoidable things can happen to cause us to be late. In such cases, just slip in quietly and listen until you catch the flow of the gathering. You do not want to enter late with a whoosh of your energy that derails the process already underway. Honor what is happening and slide in as best you can.

It will help to meet in the same place for each of the six sessions. If you rotate from one location to another, you will be distracted by the need to locate the bathroom, wonder about privacy, or decide which chair is yours. You will be more comfortable in a physical place that you know. After you have settled into one space, you will be able to relax and tend more effectively to the business at hand. It is possible to rotate from one location to another, but you will have more adjustments to make. Though the physical setting can matter, the emotional tone of the group is most important.

Learning takes time and repetition. You cannot learn these community-building skills by simply reading this book. Nor can you learn them by applying the lessons just once. You will have to practice these lessons over and over. Becoming a community-building master is a skill no less profound than becoming a martial arts master. Both take years of steady practice.

> *Tony prided himself on his ability to solve almost any problem by himself. When he decided to learn some self defense skills, Tony bought a book. But he was not satisfied with the results.*
>
> *So Tony went to a Kung Fu class and asked one of the teachers to show him some self defense moves. The teacher asked if he was willing to practice and Tony said he was, so the instructor showed Tony a particular movement and told him to work on it in the corner. Tony soon got bored and his arm became tired so he put on his shoes and left.*
>
> *A few weeks later he came back because he knew he was not learning what he wanted. The teacher again had him practice the same movement and this time Tony spent many sessions in the corner practicing until it became automatic.*
>
> *The teacher then told him to spar with other students so he could practice his new movement face-to-face. Tony was a bit of a loner and accustomed to doing most things by himself, so this was a challenge. But being determined, he swallowed his discomfort and began to spar. Soon he was developing a beginning skill level at self defense and to his surprise, a sense of fondness for his fellow students. Though they were all business with Kung Fu, the group gave Tony a sense of community.*
>
> *Tony realized he was learning what he wanted, was finding new friends and by his persistence had begun a life long learning process that would change his very nerve fibers.*

How To Gain The Most From Your Study Group Experience

If you are taking this course with others, this section is for you. First of all, treat your study circle as a closed group. That means the same people who begin together should stay together throughout the six-week series. As you go along, some of you may tell a friend who would like to join the class. Help your friend to start another group. It is important for everyone's learning that the same people stay together for the entire series. It is a little like a mountain climbing group having to stop in the middle of an ascent to train a newcomer in the skills of climbing before they continue. Bringing in new members after the first session will take too much energy from the group and will decrease how much you learn.

If you are looking for a group to work with, here are some ways to start one. You can invite a few people who you think would be interested and propose that they join together to take this course. This could be a group of friends or others who share a common situation or interest, several single moms, for example. Or you could suggest to your book group that they go through this course together. If you are lucky, you might hear about a group that is already gathering and ask to be included. You might place a small ad in your local newspaper or on a web bulletin board. Or you could ask the local community center, community college, or church to offer a class and then sign up.

When you invite people to join your study group, be selective. Some people take a great deal of energy. Some are incessant talkers who will not give room to others no matter how hard you try to have your say. These people simply take over and push everyone else to the side. Others are on some kind of personal mission—a political agenda or some belief system—and may want to impose it on you. And some people are simply very difficult. Eventually, you will need to learn how to relate to all kinds of people, but for this course, give yourself a break and choose people who have a sincere desire to share, to learn, to listen, and to work with others.

I recommend that you limit the study group to six people. Two people can take this course, though a group of between three and six is best. If your group is larger than six, it will take too much time to get around to everyone so I suggest that you break the group into study pods. Then several pods can share the same room with each group working individually. That way you can mingle with people in the other pods during the breaks. If you are part of a pod, it is best to stay with your group. As people work together, a sense of trust grows which will foster openness and receptivity in everyone. Hopping from pod to pod will interfere with the creation of that base of trust and familiarity.

A note about the timed group exercises. The times you will find in the instructions are based on a circle of six people. If you are in a pod that has fewer than six, you can give more time to each person and still stay within the overall time allowed for the exercise.

How To Gain The Most From The Individual Self-Study Process

If your situation dictates that you take this course alone, here are some tips for you.

Treat the course the same way you would a class. Show up with a steady intention to progress through a complete session in one sitting. You will not gain much by casually browsing the sessions on the bus going to work or while watching TV. Make it a point to set an hour or two aside to focus on one complete session without outside distractions.

Before you begin, scan over the lesson to make sure you have everything you will need. At a minimum, you will need a pen and a clean copy of this workbook. Then decide the place where you will take the course. You will be able to settle more deeply into the material if you choose a comfortable, pleasing spot which you can retreat to each time. This stability will give you a sense of being anchored with both the material you will be studying and the place.

In order to set the stage for what comes next, be sure you have read and understood everything in the front of the book before you begin. After you have sat down with book in hand, follow the instructions for the session you are covering. Instead of talking with a group, you will be journaling and contemplating.

Journaling is a powerful way to learn and explore yourself. And it is a tried and true way to learn. When you journal, you write down whatever comes to mind about a particular topic without planning or pre-thought. Do not edit or censor what flows onto the paper. Let yourself be surprised. That free-flow process will let you tap into a place of knowing deep inside and will bring that wisdom into your conscious awareness. In that way you will be better able to integrate what you are learning into your self knowledge.

Journaling and its close sister, free-or non-stop writing, have long been used by writers to understand what they think and observe. It is an invaluable method of tapping into your mental resources and can have a number of useful applications. In this course, you can use it to help you understand and apply what you are learning.

When you journal, you are not trying to produce a written piece for another person. No one is going to judge you or grade you on what you have written. You are having a private conversation between your daily aware self and your deepest unconscious self. As you journal, the material begins to take up residence inside of you in a deeply profound way.

Contemplation, on the other hand, is a process of turning over something in your thoughts, writing about it, and considering it from many points of view. When you contemplate, you take an idea and work with it in many ways. You are feeding your ideas and thoughts into your intuition where a new knowing can arise. Again do not censor or edit or be judgmental. You are being led to a felt sense of whatever you are focusing on. When you contemplate, let yourself be surprised by what emerges. Journaling and contemplation work hand in hand.

At the end of each session, notice that fresh ideas keep springing up. Keep your journal handy so you can write them down.

Even though you are doing this course individually, be sure to take every opportunity to interact with other people. The material in each session will suggest some ways you can do that. One way is to hang out in public places and watch people through new eyes. Another is to talk with a friend about what you are discovering. You can do this face to face or even over the Internet. The more you interact with others, the richer your experience will be.

Guardianship

Each of you is a guardian of this course. That means to:

- Keep to the structure of each session.
- Treat everyone with generosity and respect.
- Respect the privacy of everyone in the class, including your own.
- Take your turn to be the timekeeper and to gently nudge the conversations back into focus. Even if you are not the designated timekeeper, continue to hold in your mind and heart the wellbeing of everyone in the circle.
- Discipline yourself to stay with the topic in front of you if you are working alone.
- Redirect the conversation when needed. As always happens in groups, some people get so carried away with their train of thought that they forget that others also have things to say. If this happens in your group, simply say: "I want to hear from_____." Or you can say: "Excuse me, let's give_____ a chance to share."

If you are one of the talkers, know that other people may feel you are taking over and grow to resent you. Part of your guardianship will be to create room for others to share. That means sometimes sitting quietly even if you have something pressing to say. If what you have to say is really important, jot it down and you can come back to it later. Make sure that everyone has an equal time to say their piece.

- If one of the group members is holding back, inquire if they have something they want to say. If they don't want to talk at a particular time, honor that and give them space and time. But do not forget them if they decide to pass. By holding their need to sit quietly, you care for them, even if they do not participate as actively as others. We each have our own unique ways of being with people and of learning.
- Accept whatever someone shares. Resist a tendency to give advice or to correct what is said. Be totally accepting of other's thoughts and ideas and be very careful to censor your own internal critic. Being critical of others only damages relationships.

By observing good guardianship in this class, you will be learning how to be a guardian of every relationship in your life.

The Importance Of Warm-up

When you take an airplane trip, you first plan your destination, then you board the plane. Now the pilot starts the engines and lets them Warm-up. At that point, the plane begins to taxi to the end of the strip. Only then, after all these preliminary steps, do you actually accelerate down the strip, take off, and begin the serious business of the journey.

You cannot take a trip in an airplane without doing these steps. The same is true for human encounters. Even if the encounter is unexpected, there always is a period of greeting, agreeing upon some common interest, deciding what you will do together, and moving toward doing it.

Two people meet in the market. They greet each other, catch up with the news, and decide to go for coffee to have a conversation. People never just run into each other and are suddenly discussing something vitally important over a cup of coffee.

Warm-up is essential. We warm up to a wedding by going through an intensive preparation process. Weeks of organization—choosing dresses, flowers, the minister, the form of the ceremony, the guest list, and the reception details—all set the stage for the event and also warm us up so that we are at our best. The same is true of preparing and eating a meal to planning and executing a vacation. Everything needs a lead-in, a Warm-up. In the same way, the Warm-up to each session in this course is essential. Be sure to give this step careful attention and effort.

Warm-up can be many things: preparation, going over your notes, stretching before exercise, or planning a menu, to name a few. If you are not intentional about warming up, you may approach a new event with avoidance. First you sharpen the pencils. Then you call a friend. After that you read a magazine. It takes forever to get going. Instead of circling around the event like a dog about to lie down, be purposeful about creating an initial Warm-up process.

Warm-up almost always begins by anticipating or thinking about some new event or encounter. Then it involves focusing on the task at hand and holding your attention to that task until it is underway. In this class it usually means looking over your notes before you arrive, having a little social time making small talk, and then gradually turning to the business of the session.

Remember that every greeting or human event starts with a Warm-up. Being attentive to this will make you more effective in moving through your people world.

1st Session — Defining The Personal Village

Welcome To This Course

What you are about to study has the potential to change your life. You will be gaining some of the shared wisdom and knowledge practiced by billions of people over thousands of years. The ideas in this course have been taught to people in every period in history, in all walks of life, and in every imaginable situation.

Every one of us automatically takes this course if we are born into a strong family. We learn how to navigate through the waves of people who flow through our lives by simply doing it. When we dance in harmony with those around us, life takes on the richness, meaning, and satisfaction that are our birthright. Knowing how to navigate successfully in and through your personal community is one of life's core skills. This course will remind you of many things you already know and it will add some valuable new skills.

In some ways, you have been taking this course all your life without realizing it. Now you are going to bring into focus what you already know about community building and add to it. In time, you will become your own Personal Village master.

This is your people skills course. Armed with this new knowledge, you will assure yourself of a strong circle of people who will bring comfort in time of need, open doors to resources that you will need to lead a more successful life, and contribute to your health and well-being. A strong Personal Village will help you to live a longer and happier life.

If you happened to skip over the section on Warm-up on page 17 of this workbook, it would be a good idea to go back and read it now. Warm-up always happens as you enter into any interaction with another person. So, as you Warm-up for each session, the first thing to do is to allow for some social time. This could be simple greetings or more extensive time for chatting. This is where you will start in your group.

If you are taking this course by yourself, be sure to set the stage by finding an ideal place where you can journal and contemplate. It might be your bed or a favorite chair or a park or a quiet coffee shop. Take some time to create the physical setting most conducive to your process. If you can always do each step in the same location, you will be able to settle more deeply into the material.

Before you begin, be sure to have a clock—a kitchen timer will work—or a small bell that the timekeeper can ring. Also, have some object handy—a ruler, a ball, a toy, or a cup, anything that can easily be held in your hand—to use as a talking stick. Now you can begin.

As you gather for the first time, spend some time greeting each other. Though you will have ample opportunity to learn about each other later, be sure to learn everyone's name now. Name tags will help. Make sure you know where to hang your coat and where the bathroom is. This social time provides the initial grease that will smooth the way for what is to follow. When the group is ready, come together for the opening circle and begin the timed-study process.

Opening Circle—Formal Warm-up:

Group—Sit in a cozy circle where you all have enough room to hold this book in your lap and still be rather close together. Your group will get more done if you all pull in close to each other.

Choose someone to serve as the guardian for this session. The guardian will lead the group through the material of each session and keep time for each step. If you have not read the introductory material on being a guardian on page 16, this would be a good time for everyone to review it.

Individual—If you are working alone, make sure that you are well fed and exercised and ready to settle down for a couple of hours. Brew yourself a cup of coffee or tea, gather some comfort food, and take some time to settle into your special study place. Begin by reading through the instructions for today's session. Read the introductory material on Warm-up and how to get the most out of this class if you have not already done so.

❶ *First Exercise—Getting Acquainted:*

Group—The guardian reads the following out loud:

Start by introducing yourself any way you want. Share why you wanted to do this class. Share a little about your work and family and, perhaps, where you live. Use the talking stick. The simple rule is that the person holding the stick is the only one who can talk. You will each have ten minutes to talk without interruption. The timekeeper will ring a bell at the end of ten minutes. At the ring of the timer or the chime of the bell, finish your sentence and pass the stick on. It is very important that you hold to this procedure and time frame; otherwise, the group never will get done. We will have an hour total.

1st Session—Defining the Personal Village

Write class mates names, here:

Individual—In your journal, write the answer to the following questions: What drew you to do this course? What community experience do you bring to the course?

What do you hope to get out of this course?

1st Session—Defining the Personal Village

Take as along as necessary to contemplate and journal about these questions:

> What drew you to this course?

> What community experience do you bring to the course?

 **Notes**

❷ Second Exercise—Sympathy Circle:

Group and **Individual**—Give yourself 23 minutes for this exercise.

Have one of the group members read the following story out loud or read it to yourself.

The Story of Margaret

Margaret shared a recently unsettling event. She is a very successful executive who knows people all around the country. On one typical day, she had flown to an out of town meeting and returned a few hours later. Back in the office, she attended meetings with clients and staff before catching a quick dinner and dashing off to a board meeting. She finally ended her people-filled day about midnight when she left for home.

When she was about two miles from home and at the edge of her neighborhood, she was jolted out of her fatigue when a car ran into her. She quickly realized that she was OK, but her car was not. Stepping out of the car, she found the other driver was so drunk he did not know what had happened. So Margaret, the totally connected modern woman, pulled out her cell phone and called the police. Soon a fire truck arrived, followed by a police car. A report was taken, the drunk was put in the police car, and tow trucks called. As Margaret stood watching, the fire truck pulled away, the tow trucks arrived, and the policeman drove off with the drunk.

At that point it was 1:30 a.m., and she wondered how she was going to get home. She asked one of the tow truck drivers if he could drop her off, but he said it was not company policy to do that and suggested she call a cab. He was curious that the policeman did not give her a lift.

She believed that a cab at that hour would require cash and all she had was a debit card. Being ever resourceful, Margaret pulled out her trusty cell phone—the guaranteed way we all use to stay connected—and scrolled through her list of names looking for someone to call. Though she found an enormous list of people, she did not find the name of even one person in her home town that she felt comfortable to ask to come get her.

She was in a fairly safe and well-lighted neighborhood, so she walked the two miles home. At 2 a.m. she arrived at her door, exhausted, a little scared, and angry. Mostly she was very sobered because the realization had dawned on her that, in spite of all the people she knew, there was not a single name on her list that she could call in this situation. She had spent all her time building business relationships and had neglected to build a personal network of close friends.

1st Session—Defining the Personal Village

Social psychologists describe the folks that you can call upon in any situation, your Sympathy Circle. Some call it their "call circle." Take a few minutes to think about whom you could call at any time of the day or night for help in the event of an emergency.

Write down those names and add a word or two about the nature of your relationship.

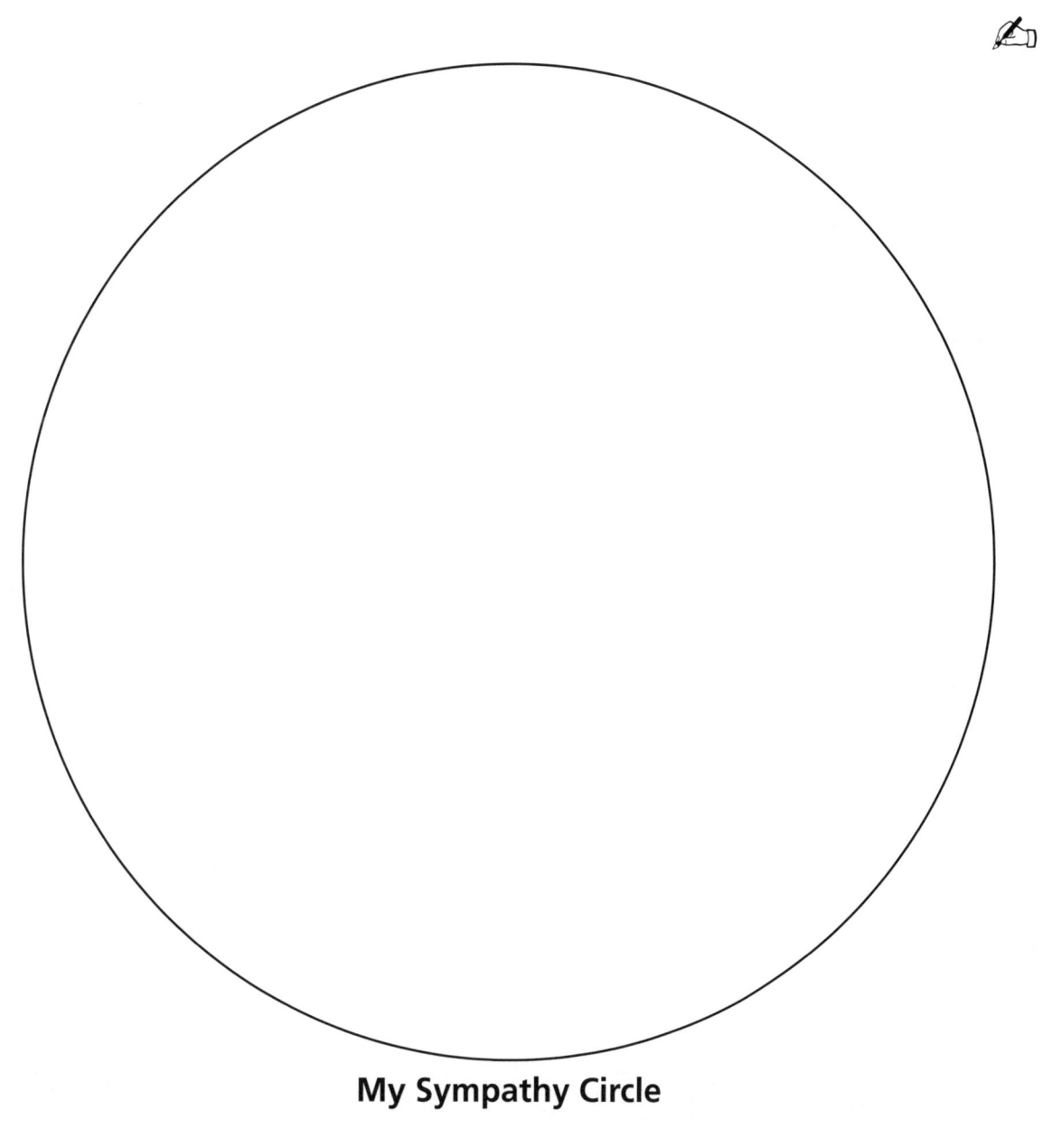

My Sympathy Circle

1st Session—Defining the Personal Village

After you have completed your Sympathy Circles, spend another 10 minutes sharing with your group (no talking stick) or, if you are doing this class individually, journal about the people in your Sympathy Circle. How many people are in it? Who are they? How many people depend upon you to be a member of their Sympathy Circle? Jot down things that occurred to you during the conversation.

Write down your thoughts about your Sympathy Circle:

❸ Third Exercise—Personal Village Inventory:

Group—The people in your Sympathy Circle are only the beginning of a much more comprehensive list you are now going to compile.

At this point, pull away a little from your study pod. Write down the names of everyone you know personally. Organize their names according to the categories below. If you have a cluster of people that does not fit into one of these categories, make a new one. If one person appears in different categories, enter the name each time it appears in a new category. The same person may inhabit different places in your Personal Village.

You will have 10 minutes. Write every name that comes to mind as fast as you can. The guardian will set the timer.

My Personal Village Inventory—Family

My most intimate family members:

All other family members:

1st Session—Defining the Personal Village

My Personal Village Inventory—Friends

My most intimate friends:

All other friends:

1st Session—Defining the Personal Village

My Personal Village Inventory—Colleagues and people at work or school

The most important:

All others:

This list contains, colleagues, fellow students, clients, professional associates, customers, study group members.

1st Session—Defining the Personal Village

My Personal Village Inventory—Folks who make my life work

Include in this list doctors, mechanics, hair dressers, teachers, and people who have valuable networks that are helpful to you.

My Personal Village Inventory—Members of any organization to which you belong

Very significant folks:

All others:

After ten minutes, come back to your circle and pair up with one or two other people. This can be frustrating because you have just begun. You will have time in the coming week to add more names. Share what has emerged so far. As you share, more clusters may come to mind and the flood-tide of names will continue to flow. Jot down some of the additional names as the others talk. You will have a total of 15 minutes to talk.

Individual—Journal about what has begun to emerge on your list. What did you notice? Are there as many people as you want? Can you see some areas where you need to expand your people list?

↪ *Closing Exercise:*

Group and Individual—In the remaining time, have an open sharing (no talking stick) or a journaling experience where you address the question: How has this session worked for me? Did I have enough time? Did I learn anything new?

Before you quit, assign one person to bring drawing supplies for next week. You will need a couple of large sheets of paper for each person and a box of crayons or felt pens. Close by thanking everyone and yourself for contributing to this experience.

↪ *After the class:*

Take some time to enter in your workbook what came up for you during the session. Were you surprised? Did you learn anything new? Did you understand what Personal Village is about? Are you left with questions? If you are working with a group, do the people in your study pod seem to be compatible? Do you think this will be a circle of people that you can work with? Write down the answers in the journal at the end of the book.

↪ *Suggestions if you want to do more before the next session:*

Finish filling out the people list and organize it into the categories. Pull out all your old Christmas card lists, personal organizers, and appointment books, and scroll through your phone list.

Read the Second Session in this workbook before the next class.

Rent the movie *Fiddler On The Roof* and watch it either alone or with other group members. This is a classic and enjoyable film depicting a romanticized version of an Eastern European village. It shows the delights and struggles of Tevye, a poor milkman, who is immersed in his Personal

Village. It is a magnificent musical showing life in all its dimensions, from simple to complex, ever-changing, ever-rich, ever-human.

Read Chapter 3 in the *Personal Village* text. If you have not yet read the first two chapters of the primary text, you could do that also.

↪ *Take the Test:*

Pick one group or a single relationship in your Personal Village and apply the Community Fulfillment Test on page 71 as a way to begin thinking about how that situation is working for you. Included with the Test is a description of what it is and how to think about it. When you interpret this Test simply let your intuition speak to you. As you go along with this course, this Test will begin to have more meaning.

2nd Session — Shaping Your Personal Village

Gathering—Informal Warm-up:

Group—During the initial social time, welcome each other with warmth and respect. Make sure you know everyone's name and ask how last week went.

Individual—Make yourself a cup of tea or go for a walk and think about what came up for you in the last week.

Opening Circle—Formal Warm-up:

- Circle together.
- Sit as close as possible while still being comfortable.
- Choose this session's guardian. Make sure the guardian is clear about his or her job.

❶ *First Exercise:*

Group—Share what came up for you since last week. Did you add to your people list? What occurred to you as the list grew? How many people do you have on your list? Do you have people in each of the different categories? Are all the people in just one or two categories? Use the talking stick and hold the time to 5 minutes for each person. You will have a total of 30 minutes.

Individual— In your journal, answer the above questions.

What has emerged for me in the last week?

2ND SESSION—SHAPING YOUR PERSONAL VILLAGE

❷ Second Exercise—Personal Village drawing:

Materials needed for the drawing exercise: A large sheet of paper for each person. Large drawing pads or butcher paper are good. A box of crayons or colored felt pens.

Group or Individual—Gather a large piece of paper and a handful of crayons. Everyone spread out in the room and find a space to draw. Using the drawing materials, create a picture of your Personal Village. That means to craft something on paper that represents all the people in your life. The picture will come from your inner creative self.

Your picture may be symbolic splotches of color or free-form shapes or a stick picture of the people in your life. Or, if you are an artist, you might create an actual work of art. Just let the picture emerge. One way to do this is to hold the intent to depict your Personal Village on paper and then simply allow the form to emerge. You may or may not know what is emerging until later. Remember that everything that comes onto the paper is uniquely yours and stands on its own without editing or criticism from you or others.

Allow 25 minutes to draw; the guardian will set the timer.

After the timer has gone off:

Gather back in the Group—Each of you will take a turn showing your picture and describing what came to mind as you drew it. After you share, other group members can comment on what they see. You have five minutes each to present your picture and receive comments. The timekeeper will allow 30 minutes.

Individual—After finishing your picture, spend some time studying it. Add a few touches as you feel moved to do so. Write in your journal anything that came up for you during this creation. Did the unique way in which you drew the picture have any meaning for you?

Thoughts about my picture:

❸ Third Exercise—Introduction to The Intimacy Continuum:

Group—Have one person read the following Introduction to The Intimacy Continuum followed by an open conversation about what springs up as you think about your Personal Village in this context. Allow 20 minutes total for this introduction.

Individual—Do the same process by journaling.

↪ *Introduction to The Intimacy Continuum*

> *The amount of intimacy that people have with you is a very important lens through which you can study the inventory you started last week. Intimacy means the degree to which two people know each other. The more you feel known by another person, the more intimacy you feel. If you want a deeper description of how intimacy works, read Chapter 3 in the primary text.*
>
> *With some people you will have very little intimacy or emotional connection. They may be the folks at the bus stop or the receptionist at the doctor's office. Some are casual acquaintances with whom intimacy is very low. Some are instrumental to your life—people who help make your life work but have very little, if any, emotional connection, like the mechanic. Some are fellow students or colleagues with whom you have had some personal sharing and knowing. This connection is more intimate. Others are your dearest beloved friends or family members. This is maximum intimacy.*

The Intimacy Continuum shown here gives you an idea.

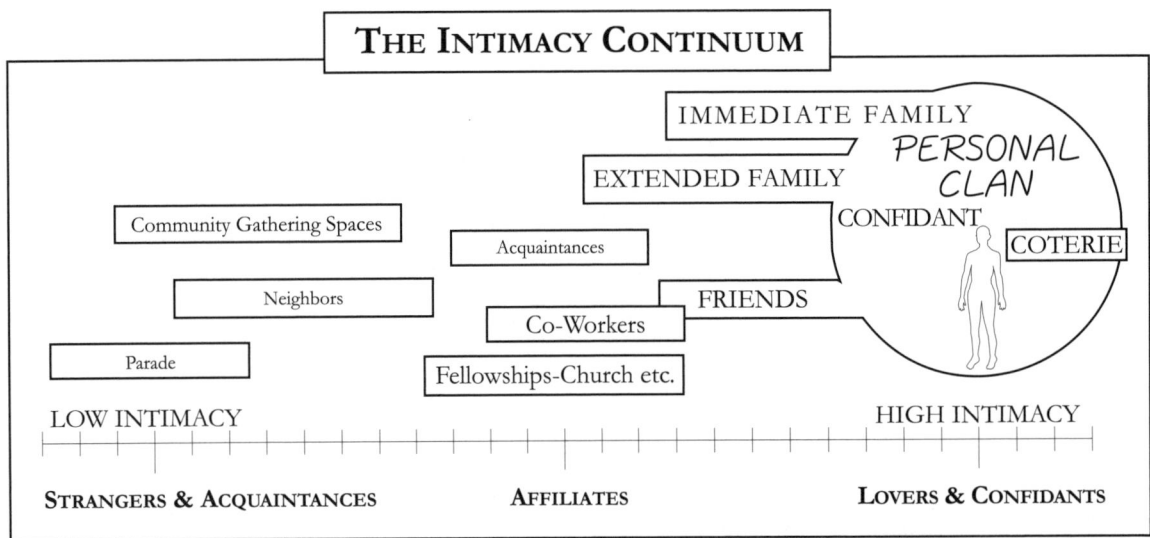

This is simply an introduction. We will discuss this idea in more detail later.

2ND SESSION—SHAPING YOUR PERSONAL VILLAGE

> Some thoughts about the Intimacy Continuum and my Personal Village: ✎

↪ Closing Exercise:

In the time remaining, consider the following questions: Did anything stand out in this session that was particularly interesting or valuable? Was the drawing exercise enlightening? Was the idea of an Intimacy Continuum new to you?

Bring your session to a close by expressing gratitude to yourself for the effort you put in and to others for their presence and contribution. If you are in a study circle, put the talking stick in the middle of the floor and have an open conversation.

↪ After the class:

In your workbook, enter ideas and impressions that emerged from this class. What happened as you drew the Personal Village picture? If you have not done so yet, go back to your picture and spend some time studying it and contemplating what inspiration springs up from what you have created. Had you ever thought about the idea of an Intimacy Continuum as a way to describe where people fit into your life? Does this seem like a useful idea at this point?

Write down what questions are emerging for you in the journal space at the end of the book.

➜ Some suggestions if you want more before the next session:

Hang your drawing up where you can look at it every day.

Practice welcoming everyone you meet with genuine warmth and respect.

Go back over the people list and reorganize it onto an Intimacy Continuum.

Create an Intimacy Continuum picture of your Personal Village that you can share with the group next week.

Go back to the Community Fulfillment Test at the end of the book and choose a relationship to examine. You could pick a friendship or a marriage or a colleague or fellow student. If you identify something in the relationship that is not totally meeting your needs, write in your journal ideas about what you could do to correct the situation.

Read Chapter 4 in the primary text.

Go through the 3rd Session before coming to class.

3rd Session—Roaming As An Art

Gathering—Informal Warm-up:

Group—Greet your group members and ask if anything interesting happened in their lives this last week. Spend a little time getting better acquainted with two or three people.

Individual—Before you begin, go for a short, brisk walk with your arms swinging in time to your gait. This will help to pattern your brain so that you will be more alert and receptive. Back at home, make yourself a cup of tea and think back over your week. Did anything interesting happen with the people in your life?

Opening Circle—Formal Warm-up:

- Circle together.
- Sit as close as possible while still being comfortable.
- Choose this session's guardian.

❶ First Exercise—Going deeper with The Intimacy Continuum:

Group—If you did any further work on The Intimacy Continuum, share what you discovered. Have a conversation about the intimacy concept and your understanding of groking. Talk among yourselves about how skilled you are at groking. Have you known about groking by another name? Give each person about 5 minutes without the talking stick, 30 minutes total.

Individual—Study the Intimacy Continuum and compare it to the people list you made the previous week. Contemplate the Continuum and your list and write down in your journal anything that occurs to you. Write your thoughts about groking. Do you feel groked by anyone? What did it feel like? How would you rate yourself on your ability to grok?

My thoughts about the degree of intimacy in my inventory:

❷ Second Exercise—Introduction to Roaming:

Group—The guardian reads out loud the following instructions:

Everyone stand up and pretend you have never met and have just come together as a group for the first time. Wander around the room and, without talking or using any words, begin to mingle as if you were in a crowd of strangers. Continue wandering for about one minute and then begin to make eye contact as you pass each other. Do that for another minute. Next, as you wander, begin to nod and smile. After another minute, start to say hello to people as you pass. Do not engage any further at this point.

After you have completed the first three steps of wandering, stop, sit down, and, without any discussion, either read or have someone read the Introduction to Roaming.

Individual—Do the above process in a church coffee hour or at school or work or even in a familiar grocery store. Be subtle about this or people will think you are strange.

↪ Introduction to Roaming

Roaming is the universal way we have always used to explore our surroundings, including our people environment. Until we get acquainted, we always start by hanging out and wandering around in our natural setting.

Developing a relationship requires a complex Warm-up that first includes sizing each other up and then slowly testing to see if you share a common ground, are mutually trustworthy, and will respect each other. That always takes time. Though it may seem that you can create an instant connection, it is not true that significant relationships happen instantly.

By hanging out in the territory of others, you give yourself and them a chance to study each other. You make yourself visible to others and yet maintain a distance. You learn from those "chance encounters" whether there is a common ground upon which you can walk. You gradually interact, testing each other constantly for trustworthiness and degrees of respect and warmth. In time, you will decide if there are common grounds and shared interests upon which you can build something further.

In the wandering exercise, you just did. You were engaging in the initial steps of the roaming process.

Group—Have a conversation about the wandering exercise. Did you feel silly or uncomfortable at first? Did the process feel familiar? Were you eager to get onto the next step of engaging with more substance? Did things begin to feel easier as you proceeded with the exercise?

Now broaden your conversation to include the general idea of Roaming. Did anything come up when you read the Roaming chapter last week? Is this an old idea to you or is it a new way to think of how to start engaging strangers? Without the talking stick, have an open conversation for 20 minutes. Be sure to give everyone time to speak.

Individual— In your journal, answer all the above questions.

My thoughts about Roaming:

❸ Third Exercise—The Principle of Seven:

Try to limit the introduction and demonstration to this topic to 20 minutes.

→ The guardian reads the following to the group:

There is a well-known tool that professionals and successful community builders use to create relationships with strangers. It is called the Principle of Seven. Studies have defined how many contacts must occur before comfort can develop between new people. According to Harvard psychologist George Miller, the average mind will keep track of the number of events up to about seven. After approximately seven events, the brain will make an internal accounting shift and lump all of the events into the category of many. The mind simply stops counting after awhile and most people experience this internal shift as "familiar." With this shift comes a sense of increased comfort.

After the seventh contact, it is almost as if the brain says," Oh, she has been around for awhile. I guess she is OK." At this point, each of you makes a psychological shift from stranger to familiar stranger or from outsider to insider. Everything gets easier.

Professionals use this method to build networks of colleagues and potential business contacts. Psychologists use it to gradually build trust and to create familiarity for resolving conflicts and negotiating contracts. Sales representatives use the Principle of Seven to build a base for more fruitful business relationships.

You can use it to transform strangers into casual acquaintances and maybe, eventually, friends and, perhaps, even into relationships that are really important. The Principle of Seven is one of your more useful people tools.

Group—Two people will demonstrate the Principle of Seven for the group.

The guardian asks two people to demonstrate the Principle of Seven while he or she guides them step by step through the enactment. The guardian will be the director by spelling out each step before the actors do it. The two actors pretend they have never met and are encountering each other for the first time in a book store. Actually this will be a combination of demonstration and improvisational theater.

> ***Step 1 First Encounter***—One person stands on one side of the room pretending to read a book. The other walks across the room, passes the reader, and looks up as he or she passes.

> ***Step 2 Second Encounter***—The first person pretends to be walking down the stack of books. The second person walks by. They look at each other and smile.

> ***Step 3 Third Encounter***—As both actors wander in the book store, they make eye contact, smile, and say "Hello."

> ***Step 4 Fourth Encounter***—One person is looking at a book. The other wanders in the store, encounters the book looker, makes eye contact, smiles, and says: "Hello. I keep running into you here. My name is _____. What is yours?" Then with a brief "It is nice to meet a fellow book lover," smile, and excuse yourself.

By this point, the demonstration may seem stiff or wooden and even a little artificial. Do not worry. It will become easier as you go along.

> ***Step 5 Fifth Encounter***—The two actors meet, make eye contact, smile, and greet each other by name.

>> Now find a way to make small talk about the book store: "What brings you here? Have you found any interesting books?"

>> After chatting a bit about the book store, ask: "What do you do in the outer world when not coming to the book store? Do you have children? Where do you work? Have you been coming here long?"

>> See how far you can go in learning something outside of the context of the store.

If you are doing this in the real world you would, be making small talk about the weather or the traffic or anything that seems obvious in the context of your being together. Be respectful. If this new person does not want to talk about a particular subject or engage any further, simply say: "It has been nice talking with you," and walk on. You may be trying to go too fast or the other person may not be comfortable. Do not push for more contact this early.

> ***Step 6 Sixth Encounter***—One person walks up to the other person in the book store and greets him or her by name, smiles, and tries to engage around something that the two have shared earlier. Make an effort to expand the conversation to things you know about each other beyond the book store. Let a conversation bloom about things that are of mutual interest. See if you can discover something about that person that you might be interested in doing together in the outer world. After a nice conversation, say "It was nice talking with you," and walk away.

You will be able to gage this meeting by how comfortable you felt in past encounters and by the signals the person is giving off about receptivity to contact. If a conversation develops, explore for common ground and the possibility of meeting at a later time around some mutual interest.

> ***Step 7 Seventh Encounter***—This time when the actors meet, use names, inquire about something learned earlier, and see if the conversation can be extended into suggesting a meeting outside of the book store—an event or a cup of coffee or ask if the other person will show you something that you are interested in.

These seven steps usually take place over a period of time, sometimes spaced out days or weeks apart. In a social event, some of these steps may be compressed into one encounter. Remember that you are only getting started in this relationship. It may never go beyond what you have developed, or it may expand and, in rare instances, turn into something meaningful.

Everyone return to the group and have a conversation about the skit without using the talking stick. If anyone is confused or has questions about the Principle of Seven, perhaps other group members can bring clarity. Allow 20 minutes for this conversation.

Individual—Read the Principle of Seven and then go out into some public place and practice it. This may take several different sessions over a few days.

Back at home, journal about how it went and what comes to mind about this technique.

What did I discover about the Principle of Seven?

↪ Closing Exercise:

Close the group by sharing what you thought and felt about today's class. Close by thanking everyone and yourself for taking part.

If you are doing this course individually, journal about the same question.

↪ After the class:

Enter in your workbook, any impressions and ideas that emerged from this class. As you pretended to wander in a group of strangers, what emerged? Was the idea of roaming new to you? Did it make sense? How have you used Roaming in the past to expand your Personal Village? Can you think of a way and place where you can roam and practice the Principle of Seven in your personal life?

Write in your journal your thoughts about Roaming and the Principle of Seven.

↪ Some suggestions if you want more before the next session:

Practice Roaming in your neighborhood and begin to experiment with the Principle of Seven.

Read the 4th session before next week's class.

Read Chapter 8 in the primary text.

4th Session— Meeting People

Gathering:

Group—By now you are beginning to know some things about the people in your group. Use your social time to greet each other and ask a couple of people about something that you have already learned about them. Remember to welcome each individual with warmth and a big smile.

Individual—Before you begin, Warm-up by Roaming in a local store or a busy park to gain the feeling of being in the company of new people. Then come home and make your tea and again think back over your week. Jot down a few things that happened in your Personal Village since the last session.

Opening Circle:

- Circle together and sit closely.
- Choose today's guardian.

❶ *First Exercise—Reviewing the past week:*

Group—Share your experience with Roaming and any discoveries since the last session. Did you have any experiences with starting the seven meetings with anyone? Each person has 4 minutes with the talking stick, 25 minutes total.

Individual—Journal about your experiences over the last week or about Roaming and contemplating using the Principle of Seven. Did you have any interesting experiences or observations?

My observations about Roaming and the Principle of Seven.

❷ Second Exercise—The art of meeting people and starting a relationship:

↪ *Read the following to yourselves:*

Some people are naturally comfortable with engaging with a new person, but for most of us, this is not easy. The very first thing to do when you want to meet a new person is to be in the same place with them. Better yet is to have something in common with this new person.

When you want to bring new people into your life, begin by hanging out where folks are doing something that is of interest to you. If you want to meet fellow Methodists, hang out at the church. If you want to meet people who are into exercise, hang out in the gym or in a yoga class. If you make the mistake, however, of hanging out where people are doing something of no interest or even disturbing to you, the potential relationships you would make there probably will not turn out well.

We have been focusing on hanging out and roaming around. And we have been working with the basic practice of showing up seven times, embracing more and more contact with each encounter. Most of the people with whom you attempt to develop a relationship will only evolve a little way along the intimacy scale. Acquaintances are usually what you get in an attempt to develop contact. Remember that all relationships initially start with strangers who become familiar strangers (people you recognize, but do not know anything about) and then become acquaintances. A few will become friends and a very few of those will become very important to us. This process takes time. And it takes persistence on our part to keep reaching out to develop a field of familiarity and trust.

↪ *Meeting people skit:*

Group—A setting where we often have a challenge in establishing contact is in a gathering of strangers, like the first day at school or a party. For this exercise, two members of your group volunteer to role play pretending you are meeting each other for the first time in a class or at a fellowship. The guardian will allow about 15 minutes for this improvisational skit.

Experiment with the tactics used in the Principle of Seven as you engage. Two of you will carry out the skit while everyone else watches without comment. If the two actors are not very successful in this pretend meeting, that is even better. You learn more from your mistakes, and the following group conversation will be rich in exploring how the conversation could have been more effective.

4th Session—Meeting People

Here is a list of questions you can use as starters for a conversation. It is OK to have the list in your hand as you do the skit. If one of the questions succeeds in starting a conversation, let that develop until that topic goes flat and then move to a new question.

- What brings you to this (class, fellowship, meeting, gathering)?
- Have you been coming here long?
- How do know your (our host)?
- Where do you live?
- Have you always lived there?
- When did you move here and where did you come from?
- Where did you go to school?
- What kind of work do you do?
- How did you get started in that kind of work?
- What do you do for fun?
- Do you know a good (doctor, dentist, mechanic, cafe)?
- Where have you traveled recently?

Individual—Go to a store, a church fellowship, or a class, and watch how people go about meeting each other. Be careful to avoid being obvious.

Group—After the role play, have a conversation where the two actors share what they experienced and then other members chime in with their observations. No talking stick. Make room for people to ask questions and gather ideas from group members. Share experiences you have had in the past with meeting people. Remember to give everyone a change to speak. The timekeeper will allow 30 minutes for this conversation.

Individual—Try this exercise yourself with a stranger in a coffee house or at school or at a church fellowship. Journal about what you felt and discovered.

4th Session—Meeting People

What did I notice about myself as I engaged with new people?

❸ Third Exercise—Being careful with new people:

→ *Everyone quietly read the following:*

As you read in Chapter 8, most people are trustworthy and will treat our efforts to make contact with receptivity. But some people are not to be trusted. They do not have our best interest at heart and usually they are sneaky about sucking us in so they can take advantage of us. This may not be an easy reality to face because it is hard to believe that others do not relate with the degree of goodwill that we carry. The truth is we live in a world with many dangers. We do not cross a busy street without some caution. And we have to be vigilant in our relationships also, particularly in the initial phase. As we grow to trust someone, we can let down our guard.

Each of you study the following checklist to see if any of the items ring a bell for you. Have you ever known someone who fits one of these descriptions? What happened in your relationship?

Group and **Individual**—After contemplating the checklist on the next page, either journal or share with your group about what emerged. In the circle, each of you will have five minutes with the talking stick, 30 minutes total.

What comes up in me when I consider that some people are dangerous?

Potentially Dangerous People Checklist

1. Do you feel somehow uncomfortable and can't put your finger on why? Your intuition is trying to tell you something. Listen, be cautious, and stay public.

2. Is this new person impulsive, lacking the patience to let things develop? Is this person in a hurry? If so, go slow.

3. Is this new person pushing you to make a decision or to take action? Back off and be careful.

4. Does he or she keep commitments? Failure to keep commitments is a red flag.

5. Does this new person exhibit nervous, agitated, or strange behavior? Inappropriate laughter or loud, fast talking is a tip-off. This is a big red flag.

6. Does the person use drugs, including alcohol, in excess? If so, he or she may be a risk to you. Be vigilant.

7. Is the person very friendly and acts as though the relationship is more intimate than your time together warrants?

8. Is there anything in this person's past behavior that is questionable, regardless of what explanations are offered? If so, proceed very carefully.

9. It bears repeating. Do you feel somehow uncomfortable and can't put your finger on why? Your intuition is trying to tell you something. Listen, be cautious, and do not go into private places with this person.

4TH SESSION—MEETING PEOPLE

→ *Closing Exercise:*

Group—Close by sharing what you thought and felt about today's class. Include any questions or unfinished issues which have emerged. Did you have enough time?

Individual—Journal about the same questions.

→ *Do this before next week:*

Create a large version of the Personal Village Map found on page 60 to bring with you next week. Choose one person to bring a few sheets of large paper for next week in case someone forgets to make a Map.

→ *After the class:*

Enter in your journal the impressions and ideas that emerged from today's session. What leapt up in you the next day or so after you thought about the idea of meeting people and the need to be careful? Can you think of ways you can be more purposeful in bringing new people into your life? Can you think of ways to protect yourself from moving too rapidly into a new relationship until you know you will be treated with respect?

→ *Some suggestions if you want more before the next session:*

Continue practicing meeting strangers and make an attempt to nourish one or two of the contacts into something positive and interesting. Begin the Principle of Seven exercise with two or three people.

Read Chapter 9 in the primary text.

5th Session—Building Friendships—Mapping Your Village

Gathering:

Group—In your social time, remember to be warm and welcoming and engage around something of mutual interest.

Individual—Before this class, Warm-up by sharing with a friend what you have been learning. Then when you sit down with your tea you will be thinking about that conversation. Your friend may have had an interesting observation that you had not considered. Jot down a few things that you have discovered in the last week. Did you have any more insights about navigating in a world where some people are to be approached with caution?

Opening Circle:

- Circle together and sit closely.
- Choose today's guardian/timekeeper.

❶ *First Exercise—What has emerged since last week?*

We have a lot to cover today, so be extra careful to stay focused.

Group—Have a conversation about what you experienced since last week when you were considering or actually reaching out to a new person. Did any surprises occur? Were you alarmed at the news that some people are dangerous? Did you think of more instances where you were taken in by someone you had first met? Did you have any experiences with engaging with a stranger? Each person has 3 minutes with the talking stick, 18 minutes total.

Individual—Journal about the same questions listed above.

5th Session—Building Friendships—Mapping Your Village

> What thoughts did I have about engaging people and the need to be careful?

❷ Second Exercise—Focusing on Friendship:

→ Everyone read to themselves and consider the following:

The purpose of a friendship:

- To give our heart a place to rest
- To support the unfolding story of our life
- To challenge us to grow and become our best
- To give us a place to play

Friendships, from the most casual to the most intimate, are essential to our success in life. It is very important to nourish our friendships in every way possible because out of that rich field of human love and support we get everything.

Ways to nourish a friendship:

- **Be courteous and gracious and treat everyone with respect.**
  Are you a courteous and gracious person?_____

- **Reach out to renew contact often.**
  Do you reach out or wait for your friend to initiate?_____

- **Nurture your friendships by expressing gratitude for large and small things.**
  Are you grateful to your friends?_____

- **Give unexpected gifts at unexpected times.**
  Are you generous with large and small gifts?_____

- **Listen rather than turn your friendship into your audience.**
  How well do you listen?_____

- **Express how much you value others by reaching out for their help.**
  The Bushmen in Africa always considered it an insult if others did not turn to them for help. By asking, you affirm that your friend has something of value to offer and thus is a person of value.
  Do you reach out to your friends for help or are you always the helper?
  _____

- **Express gratitude to your friends for who they are and what they do.**
  Do your friends know how much you appreciate them?_____

- **Give your friends an opportunity to shine.**
  Do you stand back sometimes and let your friend take center stage?
  _____

- **Say you are sorry when you hurt your friend.**
  When you hurt, insult, or slight your friend, come back and say you are sorry. We always injure our relationships inadvertently. Healing those injuries over time builds roots and depth in a friendship.
  How freely do you say "I'm sorry?"_____

- **Always welcome your friend with great warmth and caring.**
  How welcoming would you say you are?_____

Each person in the group writes the answers to the following: The guardian will set the timer for 15 minutes.

Which of the above list do you bring to your friendships?

Now answer the following question: If one of your friends was in a class like this and they were describing what kind of a friend you are to them, what do you think they would say?

Group—Break into groups of two or three. Each person has up to 5 minutes to share what friends mean to you and how much effort you put into your friendships. If you discover something about yourself that is disturbing, you can either share it or journal about it. No talking stick. The guardian will allow 15 minutes total.

Individual—After finishing the above focusing process, go for a ten minute walk, swinging your arms in rhythm with your legs. When you return, you will have patterned you brain so that you will now be able to think more deeply about the same questions posed for the group above. Journal about what comes to mind.

5th Session—Building Friendships—Mapping Your Village

❸ *Third Exercise—Personal Village Map:*

Now it is time to put your friendships into the larger perspective of your entire Personal Village. You are going to create your Personal Village Map.

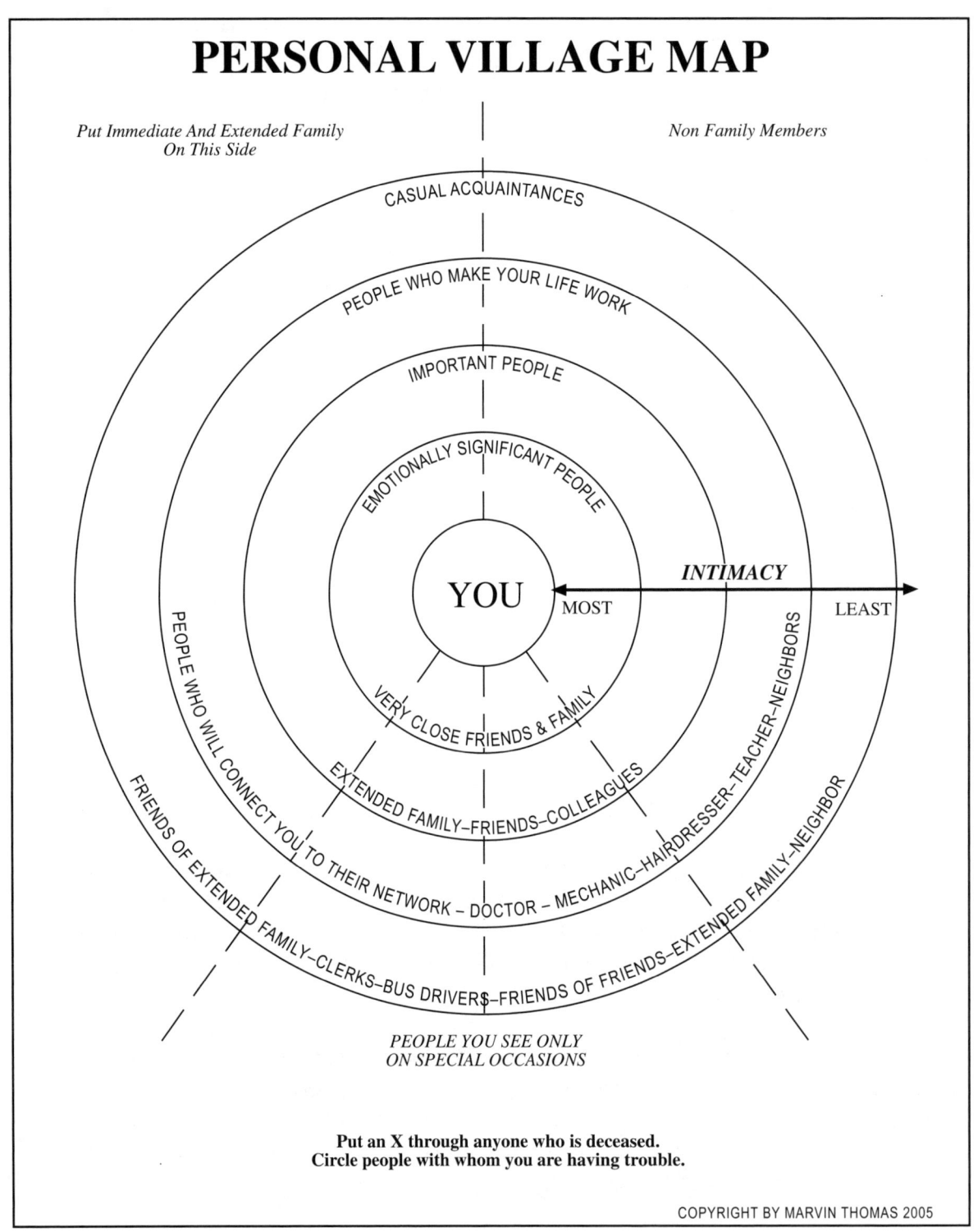

Once you have created a large version of the Map, spend 15 minutes writing in the names of all the significant people that you can think of. Go back to your people inventory in Session # 1 on page 27. Write those names in the appropriate places. Notice how the more intimate people are close to the center of the circle and those who are less intimate are toward the outside. Put immediate and extended family on the left side of the Map and everyone else on the right side. Make a big X through the name of anyone who is no longer living. Circle the names of those who make you uncomfortable or who are a problem to work with. Do not try to finish the entire Map today. Names will come to you for the next two or three days. You are just beginning.

After 15 minutes, sit back and look at your Map. This is your unique Personal Village as of today. Put a date on the Map because in a year it will be different, and you will want to see how it has changed. Study the results and ask yourself the following questions:

- Do you have as many people in each zone as you want?
- What is the balance between the number of intimate and less intimate people?
- What is the balance between the number of people in the emotionally significant circle, important people, and people who make your life work? The ideal is an even spread across the entire Map. Do you have that?

↪ *Now it is time to talk or journal:*

Group—You each have 5 minutes to present your unique Map and talk about what you saw. After sharing, group members can ask questions and add observations. Use the talking stick. Thirty minutes total.

Individual—Journal about the feelings that rose up as you did the exercise on Mapping. What new things have emerged about yourself and your Personal Village as a result of studying your Map?

5th Session—Building Friendships—Mapping Your Village

My observations about the Personal Village Map:

→ *Closing Exercise:*

Either journal or share in the circle your experience today as you considered your friendships and your Map. What emerged that was new? What did you learn about yourself?

→ *After the class:*

Enter in your journal the impressions and ideas that emerged from this class on friends. Did you have any more thoughts about the Personal Village Map? What questions do you have about the issue of friendships and your friendships in particular? Did the Map show you a new way to look at your Personal Village? What was it? Journal about what emerged.

→ *Some suggestions if you want more before next week's session:*

Write down five things you can do this week to nourish your friendships. Reach out to a friend in some special way that is unique to the two of you.

Spend more time refining your Map. Add more names. Contemplate what you saw and write down any changes or actions that would be useful for you.

Review what you have covered so far in this course.

Read Chapter 12 in the primary text.

Practice using the Relationship Evaluation Test to evaluate a couple of the relationships that you listed on your Map. You can apply this Test to a marriage or a friendship or a relationship at work. And you can use the Test to take a quick look at any small group, like work or family or church. Use the Test often enough so you can begin to see your relationships through the lens of these questions.

Relationship Evaluation Test

Pick a relationship or small constellation of relationships—a family, a church, a prayer group, a work team, or a board of directors—and rank the degree to which your personal needs are addressed in each of the following areas:

1. To what degree does this group address your needs for food, shelter, and physical safety and comfort?

   Least   1   2   3   4   5   most

2. Do you feel emotionally safe with these people?

   Least   1   2   3   4   5   most

3. How strong is your sense of belonging? Do you feel included?

   Least   1   2   3   4   5   most

4. Are your needs for human warmth, affection, and touch being met in ways which are appropriate for this group?

   Least   1   2   3   4   5   most

5. Do you have adequate opportunity to be as competent and creative as you are capable of within this circle of people?

   Least   1   2   3   4   5   most

6. To what degree do you feel personally affirmed by the people in this group?

   Least   1   2   3   4   5   most

7. How much does this person or group address your need to be involved in a greater meaning which feeds your soul?

   Least   1   2   3   4   5   most

6th Session—Pulling Your Personal Village Together

Gathering:

Group—This is your last formal session. Welcome your fellow classmates with warmth and a smile. Ask how the past week has gone and engage around some personal thing. These engagements can be quite brief.

Individual—Before you begin, Warm-up by sitting down with your workbook and scan over what you have covered. Review all the topics covered and what you have learned and written down.

Opening Circle:

- Circle together.
- Choose a guardian.

❶ First Exercise—Summing up:

Group—Sitting quietly in the circle, each of you scan the workbook and briefly review what has been covered in this course and what you discovered. After about 5 minutes, take out the talking stick. Each person will now have 5 minutes to share what has stood out for you in this course. After everyone has shared, open the conversation by asking what questions still stand. Perhaps some part of the course is still confusing or raised a whole new area of inquiry or you may have a question for a particular member of the group. The guardian will monitor the time. You will have 45 minutes total.

Individual—Follow the same steps described for the group exercise and journal about the same questions.

❷ Second Exercise—Self Reflection:

Individually reflect on how well you contribute to the people in your life. The guardian will give you 15 minutes to briefly answer the following questions:

6th Session—Pulling Your Personal Village Together

> In general how much do I purposefully give to my relationships and the people in my Personal Village?

> Am I welcoming to everyone I meet? Do I treat everyone with respect?

> Are there ways in which I neglect the important people in my life?

These questions are somewhat private. Share what feels right for you in the next exercise.

❸ Third Exercise—Discoveries and resolutions:

Take a stretch break for a few minutes. Walk around the room. Now return to your place and quietly write down the discoveries and resolutions that have emerged from this class. Allow 15 minutes total for the stretch and writing.

> What have I learned in this class that was of value to me and what do I want to do differently to nourish my Personal Village?

Group—Share what has emerged for you out of this course and any decisions you have made about how to proceed differently. Each of you will have 5 minutes with the talking stick. You will have 30 minutes total.

Individual—Journal about the same.

↪ Closing:

In the time remaining, share how this group has worked for you. No talking stick. Talk about how the experience in the circle has in some ways been a practice for what you have been learning.

It is time to say goodbye. Even though some of you may see each other again, it is always a good idea to assume that something may happen and this is your last time together. The best way to hold this possibility in your heart is to say goodbye to every person who is important to you as if you were not going to see them again. Express your gratitude and good feelings toward them as you part. A simple statement like, "I love you" or even a heartfelt warm parting like a wave or a smile is all it takes. Then you are set up for a good meeting the next time. And in the remote chance that you will not see each other again, caring is in the air. That helps everyone.

Pass around a sheet for names, phone numbers, and e-mail addresses. Have one person agree to distribute it to everyone.

↪ After the class:

Summarize in your journal what has emerged for you during these six sessions. Write down any decisions that you have made.

What To Do Next

Live the rest of your life with abundance and grace. That means doing everything you can to take care of your health, embrace your creativity, nourish all your relationships, and, ultimately, discover and pursue your purpose in life. To make this happen, you will need to apply the skills of maintaining your Personal Village for as long as you live.

What you learned in this course is essential to your physical and mental health. In fact, it is essential to the mental and physical health of everyone you know. You can only build your Personal Village by steady practice. Many people live their lives by default, waiting for others to come to them. Too often that is a mistake, resulting eventually in a very weak Personal Village. Teach yourself how to be purposeful and proactive in drawing new relationships to you and then nourishing them as if your life depended upon it, because it does.

If you have not already done so, read the text, *Personal Village,* and study the resources listed there.

Take your life and all your relationships seriously. Your Personal Village is one of the most important assets you have in your life. From the spring-board of this circle of people comes everything else.

Make it a point to give your relationships time. Drive-by connections with the important people in your life simply do not work.

↬*Here are my suggestions:*

- If you decide to continue the momentum of the course, make some time to discuss what form your continuation may take. Reading the Coterie chapter together and discussing it would be a good beginning for continuing. Some ideas you might consider are a monthly gourmet meal party, or you could start a book discussion circle focusing on the books and films recommended in the primary text. Meeting once a month for three hours is a good rhythm.

- Make sure your total Personal Village is balanced across the entire intimacy spectrum. That means bringing new people into your Personal Village on a steady basis, nourishing those relationships, letting go of the ones who leave, and finding others to take their place. You will have to put effort into making your Personal Village Map be fully balanced and satisfying.

- Make sure you have a strong circle of friends. Study the chapter on Friendship and read some of the suggested books and watch the recommended films.

- Consider steps you could make to strengthen your family. Traditional rituals, like birthdays, are a good place to start. Call or visit your family members often.

- If you do not have a strong immediate family, read Chapter 11 in the text. An intentional or alternative family can be a strong center for your Village.

- Start a coterie if you do not already have one. You could start one with your friends or the members of the study group. A group of between 4 and 6, but not more than 8, is about right for a coterie. If you do not know how get one started, study the chapter on coterie. An absolutely must read for any coterie is Christina Baldwin's book, *Calling The Circle*. It is a sterling guide.

- Make it a habit to greet every person you meet with warmth and respect. Treat every person as you would treat a customer if you worked in a doctor's office or as a bank teller. Some people will be cranky. Treat them with warmth and caring anyway.

- Talk up the idea of Personal Village to all your friends. The more this idea circulates among the people around you, the more likely it is that the germ of community will incubate and grow.

- Encourage your friends to take the Personal Village course. The wider this idea spreads that people can be caring and supportive toward one another, the stronger will be the core of our society. We all benefit.

- Become an asset to the people in your Personal Village. They are as hungry for community as you are. Your wisdom and warmth will be an inspiration to everyone around you.

- Contact me with questions or to share your own Personal Village stories. I can be reached through the web site: *personalvillage.com*.

- Check the *personalvillage.com* web site from time to time. We will be adding new material as it comes available.

May your life be full and satisfying
May you become a Personal Village master
May you dance with the greatest that you can become

Seattle 2006

Community Fulfillment Test

Community is the greenhouse within which the flower of humanity blossoms.

Community happens any time people gather together to support and nurture one another. If we think of community as a greenhouse, we need to look inside to see what is happening which allows the flowers to bloom.

One way to look at community is to evaluate how well the communal system is meeting the basic needs of every single individual involved.

Those needs are

1. Food, shelter, and the assurance of physical integrity.
2. Feeling emotionally safe.
3. Belonging.
4. Regular human warmth and affection.
5. Feeling competent with our native skills.
6. Affirmation of who we are and what we do well.
7. Involvement in a greater meaning which feeds our soul.

These needs are not luxuries. They are absolutely essential if each individual and the group as a whole are to thrive.

When the community system is providing each of the above essential needs, the people will be happy and able to function at their best. It is the responsibility of each community member to assure that every single person is given the opportunity to attain each of the seven essentials, at least to some degree.

Use the Community Fulfillment Test as a starting place to begin your evaluation of the particular grouping of people you wish to understand better. This Test can be applied to a relationship, a work team or a class, an entire organization, or a whole city. The Test is a starting place for a more comprehensive discussion.

Pick a small community cell which you belong to—a relationship or family or a church or a prayer group or a work team or a board of directors—and rank your degree of fulfillment in each of the following areas:

1. To what degree does this group address your needs for food, shelter, and physical safety and comfort?

   Least   1   2   3   4   5   most

2. Do you feel emotionally safe with these people?

   Least   1   2   3   4   5   most

3. How strong is your sense of belonging? Do you feel included?

   Least   1   2   3   4   5   most

4. Are your needs for human warmth, affection, and touch being met in ways which are appropriate for this group?

   Least   1   2   3   4   5   most

5. Do you have adequate opportunity to be as competent and creative as you are capable of within this circle of people?

   Least   1   2   3   4   5   most

6. To what degree do you feel personally affirmed by the people in this group?

   Least   1   2   3   4   5   most

7. How much does this person or group address your need to be involved in a greater meaning which feeds your soul?

   Least   1   2   3   4   5   most

Journal

Journal

Journal

Journal

Journal

Journal